The Weight of Silence

A Memoir of Childhood Trauma, Survival, and Reclaiming Your Voice

The Weight of Silence

A Memoir of Childhood Trauma, Survival, and Reclaiming Your Voice

RJ Koehler

© 2025 RJ Koehler

All rights reserved. No part of this book may be reproduced, stored in a retrieval system, or transmitted in any form or by any means—electronic, mechanical, photocopying, recording, or otherwise—without the prior written permission of the author, except for brief quotations used in reviews or scholarly works.

This book is a work of nonfiction/memoir. Names, characters, and incidents are used with discretion to protect privacy.

Copyright registered with the U.S. Copyright Office.

Self-published in Northern Pennsylvania, United States.

ISBN-13:

- eBook: 979-8-9945005-0-7
- Paperback: 979-8-995005-1-4
- Hardcover: 979-8-9945005-2-1

Printed in the United States of America.

First Edition

Dedication

For my husband,
who stood beside me when my voice was
quiet and never asked me to be anyone
other than who I am becoming.

And for my children,
you are the reason I chose healing,
the reason I chose truth, and the reason I
chose to keep going.

You've helped make this possible.

"I can be changed by what happens to me. But I refuse to be reduced by it."—Maya Angelou

Contents

Prologue — 1

Chapter 1 — When Hope Moved In 7

Chapter 2 — Learning the Rules Without Being Taught 13

Chapter 3 — The Nights I Didn't Wake Up 20

Chapter 4 — The Language of Confusion 26

Chapter 5 — When Love Becomes Conditional 32

Chapter 6 — The Secret My Body Learned First 38

Chapter 7 — The Decision Already Made 45

Chapter 8 — The Fear I Learned to Carry 52

Chapter 9 — Becoming Who I Needed To Survive ... 58

Chapter 10 — Silence as a Second Skin 64

Chapter 11 — Trust, Intimacy, and the Echoes 70

Chapter 12 — The Myth of Family Unity 77

Chapter 13 — The Moment the Story Changed 84

Chapter 14 — Naming What Was Done To Me 91

Chapter 15 — Releasing the Responsibility I Never Owned 97

Chapter 16 — Speaking Without Permission 103

Epilogue — Owning My Story 108

Acknowledgments 112

Resources — Support, Therapy, and Education 116

Author's Note — 125

Author's Intent Note —Why This Story Is Told This Way 127

References 130

About the Author 132

Prologue —

Silence is not the absence of sound. It is something that fills a room.

I learned this long before I had words for it: long before I understood that silence could be taught, enforced, and passed down like an inheritance. In our house, silence lived in the walls, settled into the furniture, waited patiently in the space between questions and answers. It showed up whenever the truth came too close to the surface.

Silence was the rule that was never written down.

From the outside, our family looked assembled, complete. Holidays photographed. Dinners were eaten at the same table. A story could be told cleanly if no one looked too closely. I learned early that appearances were not just important, they were sacred. They were something to be protected at all costs.

Even at the cost of a child.

When people talk about trauma, they often imagine a single moment, a clear before and after. But for me, the damage was cumulative. It came from what was taken, yes, but more devastatingly from what was demanded afterward. I was not just hurt; I was instructed. I was taught how to behave in the aftermath of harm. I was told what mattered and what didn't. I was told who would be protected and who would be sacrificed to keep the peace.

I was told to be quiet.

I didn't understand then that silence could be weaponized. That it could be framed as love. That adults could ask a child to carry something unbearable and call it loyalty. All I knew was that my body no longer felt like mine, and my voice no longer belonged to me.

I learned how to disappear without leaving.

Silence taught me how to split myself in two: the part that functioned and the part that remembered.

The part that smiled and the part that stayed awake at night, cataloging every wrong step, every misplaced breath, every way I might accidentally let the truth escape. I became careful. I became compliant. I became very good at reading the emotional weather of a room before speaking, if I spoke at all.

What I did not become was safe.

For years, I believed the story I was given: that I was responsible for other people's happiness, that my pain was dangerous, that telling the truth would destroy everything. I believed that love was proven by endurance, that family meant silence, and that survival required self-erasure.

These beliefs followed me into adulthood. They shaped my relationships, my sense of worth, the way I occupied space in the world. Long after the house changed and the family fractured in quieter ways, the silence remained. It settled into my bones. It spoke for me when I couldn't.

I wrote this book because silence eventually failed.

Not all at once. Not dramatically. It failed slowly, the way lies do, through exhaustion, through the weight of years, and through the quiet realization that carrying what was never yours will eventually break you. It failed the moment I understood that protecting others had never protected me.

What you are about to read is not a story of spectacle. There are no graphic scenes here, no sensational details offered for consumption. This is a story about the aftermath, about the long shadow cast by secrets, about the damage done when adults choose comfort over courage, and about the cost of asking a child to put everyone else first.

It is also a story about reclaiming what was taken.

Voice does not always return as a shout. Sometimes it comes back as a whisper. Sometimes, as a refusal. Sometimes, as a single sentence written down after years of believing you were not allowed to speak at all.

I write this for the child who learned silence too early. For the adult who carried it too long. For anyone who was told that telling the truth would ruin everything, and believed it.

This is what happens when the silence is finally set down.

Chapter 1 – When Hope Moved In

My sister and I sat at the small kitchen table, our feet swinging beneath chairs that didn't quite fit us yet. I was eleven. She was nine. The house smelled like leftovers and routine, something reheated, and something familiar. The adults stood while they talked, already halfway into a future that had been decided.

There would be more people now. More voices. More children. We were told this would be good for us and that we wouldn't feel alone anymore. As if we had been. As if loneliness was what needed fixing.

I nodded, not because I had learned to be quiet, but because I was used to being heard. I was the oldest, comfortable speaking first, and my sister followed. We hadn't yet learned to disappear into the background; we were still expressive, still sure that our reactions mattered. The adults watched our faces closely, and at the time, that attention felt like care, like something that made the path ahead smoother.

The details came in pieces. There were three boys. They were close in age. They were louder than we were, more comfortable taking up space. They weren't cruel, just unfamiliar. And unfamiliar felt enormous when you were still learning where you fit.

For a while, all of us lived together in an apartment that felt temporary even as time passed. Boxes stayed half unpacked. Furniture was arranged for function, not comfort. The days were crowded. Mornings overlapped. Evenings rubbed sharp edges into everyone. We learned who woke angry, who cried easily, and who slammed doors without meaning to.

We were told it was only for now.

A house was coming. A real one.

The house was bigger than anywhere we had lived before. Quiet in a way the apartment never was. Heavy with doors that closed completely. The adults stayed on the first floor, their room tucked away behind a boundary we were expected to respect. Upstairs belonged to the children. That separation was framed as freedom. Independence. Trust.

"You'll have your own space," we were told, as if space itself could protect us.

Upstairs, the rooms lined a narrow hallway. My sister and I shared one bedroom. The boys shared another. Between us was a bathroom that belonged to all of us, one sink, one mirror, toothbrushes pressed together in a crowded cup. We argued about messes and time and whose turn it was to clean hair from the drain. Ordinary things. Family things.

And then there was the attic.

No one explained it. We discovered it the way children do, by opening doors adults rarely thought about. Inside each bedroom closet, behind hanging clothes and storage boxes, was a small door. Those doors led to the same place: a narrow attic space that connected the two rooms.

At eleven, it seemed interesting. Almost magical. A secret passage. Something from a book. I didn't yet understand how often adventure and danger share the same doorway.

No one locked the doors. No one warned us. The attic was simply there, folded quietly into the architecture of the house.

From the outside, it worked.

We had a house. We ate dinner together. The adults seemed relieved, lighter, as if a long strain had ended. There was laughter. There were plans. The future was spoken about with confidence.

The house became a promise: space, order, and permanence, a solid thing meant to turn us into a real family instead of a group of people learning how to coexist. When it finally came, it felt like confirmation that everything was unfolding exactly as it was supposed to. I watched carefully, old enough to sense that this happiness was delicate, something that could fracture if handled too roughly. I didn't yet know how much responsibility I would take on to protect it, only that this life had been offered to us as hope, and hope felt like something you weren't allowed to question. I didn't know then that unquestioned hope can teach children to overlook danger.

At night, the house settled into sounds I didn't yet understand, pipes shifting, footsteps below, and doors opening and closing. Upstairs, we learned how to fall asleep with other people breathing on the other side of the walls.

I stayed awake longer than my sister, listening. Mapping the sounds. Learning the shape of a place that was meant to be home.

This was the beginning. The part of the story where safety still looked convincing. Where hope had not yet learned how fragile it could be. I would spend years trying to understand why my body never believed what my eyes were being shown.

Chapter 2 – Learning the Rules Without Being Taught

Every house has rules. The most important ones are rarely spoken, and they are the hardest to break.

No one ever sat us down to explain how things worked in the new house. There was no conversation about boundaries or expectations beyond the obvious: homework before television, shoes by the door, and lights out at a reasonable hour. But rules existed all the same. They always do. The most important ones just aren't spoken aloud.

I learned the rules the way children do, by watching what earned approval and what made adults uncomfortable. I adjusted myself before anyone asked, learning early that harmony was rewarded and questions were not. Over time, those rules stopped feeling external. They became internal instructions, shaping what felt safe to say, think, or feel.

Happiness, I learned, was something my mother needed to be protected.

She had waited a long time for this life. I could see it in the way she moved through the house, touching walls as she passed, standing a little taller when visitors complimented the space. She wanted this to work. She needed it to. And because I loved her and because I was the oldest, I began to understand that my role was to help keep everything running smoothly.

This wasn't said outright. It didn't have to be. Children are excellent translators of emotional subtext.

If someone was upset, we were encouraged to "let it go." If there was conflict, it was framed as a misunderstanding. If something felt wrong but didn't have a clear name, it was easier not to mention it.

Harmony was rewarded. Discomfort was inconvenient. I didn't yet understand that these rules would later be used to explain why certain questions could never be asked.

The boys were louder than we were, rougher around the edges, used to taking up space in ways my sister and I had never been allowed to. When they wrestled in the hallway or argued over the bathroom mirror, it was brushed off as normal. That's just how boys are, the adults said, smiling like this was something to be admired.

My sister and I adapted. We learned to wait our turn, to retreat rather than compete, to make ourselves smaller when the upstairs felt crowded. I learned to speak carefully, to measure my words before letting them out, to sense when now was not the time.

There were moments, small ones, when I felt uncertain, when something didn't sit right, and I couldn't explain why. But uncertainty didn't feel like something I was allowed to have. I didn't yet know how to trust it. I only knew how to override it.

The house itself taught me things, too.

Upstairs belonged to the children, but it didn't feel equally ours. Sound traveled easily through the hallway. Doors opened and closed. The shared bathroom meant shared routines, shared schedules, shared interruptions. Privacy was thin, something you negotiated rather than assumed.

The attic doors remained mostly unspoken, like an odd architectural quirk everyone pretended was unimportant. I noticed them more than anyone else did. I noticed how easy they were to open. I noticed how little attention the adults paid to them. I told myself they were nothing. Because nothing is easier to live with than something you don't have language for.

At night, when the house grew quiet, I lay awake listening again. Listening became second nature. I learned the difference between footsteps and floorboards settling, between voices drifting and doors closing. I learned how to stay very still. How to breathe quietly. How to take up as little space as possible, even in my own bed.

No one told me to do this. I just did.

Adults often talk about childhood as a time of innocence, but what they mean is ignorance. Children notice everything. We just don't always understand what we're noticing. We sense shifts in tone. We feel when expectations change. We absorb rules the way we absorb language, through immersion, repetition, and correction.

The most important rule I learned was this: don't make things harder. Don't ask questions that create discomfort. Don't name feelings that complicate the story. Don't draw attention to yourself when attention might upset the balance.

I didn't know yet what that balance would cost me. I only knew that keeping it felt like my responsibility. That being good meant being quiet. That love, in this family, was something you earned by not disrupting the peace.

By the time I realized I was living by rules no one had ever spoken, my body had already learned the cost of breaking them.

Chapter 3 — The Nights I Didn't Wake Up

This is where my memory fails, but my body does not.

I had always been a light sleeper. Before that night, I woke at everything: the click of a hallway light, the murmur of voices downstairs, and my sister shifting in her bed beside mine. Sleep was something I hovered in rather than surrendered to, one ear always tilted toward the dark.

That is how I know this night was different. I went to bed the way I always did. Clothes from that day were in the hamper. A book was placed face down on the nightstand. The small rituals that made me feel prepared, protected. My sister was already asleep, her breathing slow and even, the sound of it familiar enough to be comforting.

The house settled around us.

What I remember next is not a moment but a gap. There was no clear waking. No sharp alarm of fear. Just a sense, later, much later, that something had happened without my permission. That time had passed without my awareness. That my body had been present for something my mind had not allowed itself to know.

When I opened my eyes, the room looked the same. Darkness pressed against the edges. The ceiling fan traced slow, predictable circles. Nothing appeared disturbed, and yet everything felt wrong. I lay still, inventorying myself the way you do after a bad dream, except there was no dream to point to. Just a heaviness. A confusion that sat deep in my chest.

My body felt unfamiliar. Not injured, not visibly changed, just other. As if it had been moved without me.

I didn't have language for this. I didn't even have fear yet. Fear requires clarity, and clarity was the one thing I didn't have. Instead, there was a dull sense of disorientation, like waking in the wrong room and needing a moment to remember where you are.

I told myself I must have slept more deeply than usual. That was the most reasonable explanation. Children are taught to look for reasonable explanations first, especially when the alternative feels unthinkable.

The next day passed normally: school, homework, and dinner. The ordinary rhythm of life continued as if nothing had shifted. I watched my mother laugh. I watched the boys argue. I watched my sister chatter about her day. No one noticed anything different about me.

That night, I went to bed earlier. I don't know why. Maybe some part of me wanted distance from the day. Maybe some part of me wanted to test whether the unease would fade if I pretended hard enough that nothing was wrong.

I slept.

Again, I woke with the same sensation, the same hollow confusion, and the same sense of time missing. This time, panic fluttered briefly at the edge of my awareness, then disappeared just as quickly. My mind did something efficient and merciful. It closed a door.

Children are adaptive. It's how we survive.

After the third night, I stopped expecting myself to wake up. My body had learned what my mind could not afford to know. Sleep became a place where awareness dimmed, where questions dissolved before they could fully form.

In the mornings, I moved carefully. I paid attention to my sister, was she unchanged, still safe? I told myself that if she was fine, then everything must be fine. That was another rule I learned without being taught: if no one else is reacting, then nothing has happened.

I didn't tell anyone. Not because I had made a decision, but because I couldn't yet see what there was to tell. I had no memory to offer, no clear accusation, no words that felt solid enough to carry the weight of what my body knew.

What I had instead was a new understanding, quiet and wordless: that waking up was not guaranteed. That awareness was something the mind could withdraw. That sleep, once a refuge, could also be a place where things happened without me.

Those were the first nights I didn't wake up.

They would not be the last.

What I didn't know then was that my body was learning how to survive without my permission.

Chapter 4 – The Language of Confusion

Confusion has its own grammar.

It speaks in half-thoughts and contradictions, in questions that dissolve before they can be finished. It sounds like *maybe* and *probably,* and *I must have imagined it*. It is fluent in self-doubt and distrusts certainty the way it distrusts danger, by pretending neither exists.

Confusion is not accidental. It is what remains when the truth has nowhere safe to land.

After those nights, confusion became my primary language.

I tried to interrogate my own memories, but there was nothing solid to hold onto. No clear images. No sequence of events. Just sensations that didn't belong to any story I knew how to tell. My body reacted in ways I didn't understand. I felt jumpy for no obvious reason. I flinched at sounds that used to mean nothing. I began to dread nighttime without knowing why.

During the day, I watched myself from a distance.

I noticed how carefully I moved through the house, how aware I was of doorways, staircases, and the narrow hallway upstairs. I avoided certain spaces without making a conscious decision to do so. I felt relief when my sister was close and tension when she wasn't. I told myself these were coincidences. I had become good at telling myself things.

Adults often assume children will speak up when something is wrong, but that assumes children understand *what* is wrong. It assumes we have the vocabulary for it. I didn't. What I had instead was a collection of mismatched signals, my body saying one thing, my environment insisting on another.

Nothing looked wrong.

The house was the same. The routines were the same. The adults were the same. If I tried to imagine telling my mother that something felt off, I immediately ran into a wall of impossibility. *What would I say?* That I felt strange? That I didn't always wake up? That I was afraid of something I couldn't see or remember?

Fear without an object is easy to dismiss. I dismissed it myself.

At that age, I still believed that adults knew things children didn't, that they could see dangers invisible to us. If something truly bad were happening, surely someone would notice. Surely there would be a sign I could point to, a rule I could break, a sentence that would make sense out loud.

Instead, there was only this quiet unraveling inside me.

I began to blame myself for the confusion. Maybe I was dramatic. Maybe I was sensitive. Maybe this was just what growing up felt like, and no one had warned me. I watched other kids at school, searching for the same unease, the same heaviness. They seemed lighter. I concluded the difference must be me.

Confusion also taught me how to be silent more convincingly. I learned how to answer questions automatically. How to say "fine" and mean "stop asking." How to smile without revealing anything underneath.

It began to shape the way I understood myself. If I couldn't trust my own perceptions, then other people's versions of reality must be safer. More reliable. I learned to defer to them.

The language of confusion does not announce itself. It seeps in slowly, replacing clarity with compliance. It convinces you that not knowing is a personal failure rather than a survival response. It teaches you to doubt the one source you should be able to rely on, yourself.

At night, lying awake before sleep took over, I sometimes tried to remember everything that had happened since we moved into the house. I replayed ordinary moments, searching for something that would explain the way my body felt now. But memory refused to cooperate. It offered me only fragments and then retreated again.

Eventually, even the effort of trying felt dangerous. Questioning threatened the fragile sense of normalcy that everyone else seemed invested in maintaining. So I stopped pushing. I let the confusion settle.

I did not yet understand that confusion was not the absence of truth. It was the result of it being buried too deeply to reach.

I thought confusion meant I didn't understand. What it really meant was that understanding had been made dangerous.

I only knew this: something had changed, and I did not have the words for it. So, I learned to live without words. That silence would soon become something I was praised for.

Chapter 5 — When Love Becomes Conditional

Love didn't disappear all at once.

It shifted.

At first, the change was subtle, easy to mistake for growing pains or the normal strain of a household suddenly crowded with too many people and not enough space. But over time, I began to feel it: an invisible line I was careful not to cross, a quiet calculation I performed before speaking, moving, needing.

Love, I learned, was safest when I asked for nothing.

My mother was busy in ways she hadn't been before. There were more schedules to manage, more lunches to pack, more conflicts to smooth over. She was tired, though she rarely said so. When she did, it came with a smile, as if exhaustion were proof that she was doing something right.

"We're a family now," she reminded us often. "Families make sacrifices."

I took that sentence seriously. I took it personally.

I began to understand that her happiness was fragile, dependent on everything holding together. The marriage. The house. The image of us all functioning as we were supposed to. I could sense how badly she needed this life to work, how much she had invested in it. And somewhere along the way, I decided that my job was not to be the reason it failed.

Affection came easiest when I was agreeable, when I helped without being asked, when I didn't complain, when I didn't need reassurance or explanation. Praise followed compliance. Approval followed silence.

I watched what happened when tension surfaced, how quickly it was redirected, minimized, and reframed. Problems were treated like inconveniences, not warnings. If something threatened the calm, it was smoothed over rather than examined. I learned that discomfort was unwelcome, especially if it didn't come with a clear solution. This was not discipline. It was training.

So, I stopped bringing mine forward.

There were moments when I almost did, moments when words pressed hard against my throat, when I imagined telling my mother that something was wrong, that I felt different, unsettled, and afraid in ways I couldn't explain. But even in imagination, I could see the outcome: the confusion in her face, the fear beneath it, the way my words would ripple outward and disturb everything she was trying to hold steady.

I couldn't do that to her.

That belief took root quietly and grew fast: My needs are negotiable. Other people's stability is not.

I became careful in ways that felt necessary rather than chosen. I learned how to read my mother's moods the way sailors read weather, adjusting my behavior to avoid storms. When she was happy, I stayed light. When she was stressed, I stayed quiet. When she needed reassurance, I offered it without being asked.

Love, I realized, had terms.

It was given freely when I made things easier. It withdrew slightly when I made things complicated. It felt warm, but conditional, like something that could be taken away if I misstepped.

No one ever threatened me with that loss. No one had to. The possibility alone was enough.

Children are excellent at protecting the people they love, even when it costs them something they can't yet name. I didn't see my behavior as self-sacrifice. I saw it as maturity. Responsibility. Proof that I was good.

But something in me was shrinking.

I stopped expecting comfort. I stopped assuming I would be noticed. I stopped believing that love included space for fear or confusion or need. Instead, I treated those things like personal failures, evidence that I was not trying hard enough to be what was required of me.

This is how love becomes conditional without ever being declared so.

It doesn't arrive as cruelty. It arrives as an expectation. As gratitude that must be earned. As affection that flows more easily when you stay quiet.

I didn't yet know how much this lesson would shape the rest of my life, how often I would confuse endurance with devotion, silence with strength, and self-erasure with love.

I only knew that I was learning how to be loved by disappearing, one small piece at a time.

Chapter 6 – The Secret My Body Learned First

This is the moment everything else in this book circles back to. Not because it was the only harm, but because it taught my body what silence would cost, and what obedience would require. What happened here did not stay contained in time. It echoed forward into my sense of safety, my understanding of choice, and the way I would later confuse endurance with strength. This was not just an event. It was an instruction.

My body knew before I did.

At first, the changes were small enough to dismiss: fatigue that clung to me no matter how much I slept, a heaviness I couldn't explain, and a sense that something inside me was no longer following the rules I understood. I was a teenager. Bodies change. That explanation was readily available, and I took it. It allowed me to stay quiet. It gave my unease somewhere to hide.

But this was different.

My body began speaking in a language I didn't yet know how to translate. Signals surfaced quietly but persistently, each one carrying a weight I couldn't name. I felt unsettled in my own skin, as if something had crossed a boundary without my permission, not because I understood what was happening, but because I didn't.

I had already learned that not knowing was safer than asking. That silence preserved stability. That curiosity could fracture things that seemed too fragile to withstand it.

When the truth surfaced, it did not arrive gently. It came abruptly, wrapped in clinical language and urgency. There was a room that felt too bright. A shift in tone that made it clear something serious had been discovered. Suddenly, my body stopped being mine and became a situation: something to be addressed, corrected, and contained.

No one asked how I felt about what my body had revealed. There was no space for fear, confusion, or grief. Those emotions were inconvenient. What mattered was resolution. Control. Ensuring that what had been uncovered did not travel any farther than it already had.

I was informed of what would happen next.

Not invited into the decision.

Not consulted.

Told.

The language was calm, measured, even reassuring, as if tone alone could replace consent. I was told it was necessary. That it was the best option. That there were stakes involved, consequences larger than me. I understood, without details, that my body had created a risk, not only to myself, but to something others were trying desperately to protect.

The message settled quickly and completely:

What was happening inside me had the power to destroy everything.

What followed exists in my memory not as images, but as absence. My mind stepped away the way it had learned to do when staying present was unsafe. I remember feeling very small. I remember being handled with efficiency. I remember adults speaking around me, above me, making decisions as if my presence were incidental. This is how harm becomes invisible, by being explained instead of questioned.

When it was over, something closed.

My body returned to something that resembled normal. I did not. It no longer felt private. It felt watched. Regulated. Capable of betrayal. I learned to distrust it, to separate from it, to treat it as something that required management rather than care.

The secret did not end there.

It multiplied.

I was told never to speak of what had happened. Not to friends. Not to teachers. Not to anyone. The reasoning was presented as fact, not cruelty: people wouldn't understand. It would cause harm. It would be my responsibility if things fell apart.

I believed this.

From that moment on, my body carried evidence that my voice was forbidden to name. Every sensation felt like a liability. Every memory was a threat. I learned to police myself relentlessly, to keep my expressions neutral, my thoughts contained, my body under constant control.

This was the secret that rewrote me.

It taught me my body was not mine. That pain could be negotiated away. That survival depended on cooperation.

It taught me that silence was not optional, it was required.

I didn't yet have the language or strength to question any of this. I only knew something irreversible had happened, and that the cost of speaking had been made unmistakably clear.

So I carried the secret.

And it carried me forward into a version of myself shaped by fear, compliance, and the belief that my body existed to serve needs other than my own.

Chapter 7 – The Decision Already Made

Afterward, people spoke to me as if a decision had been made together.

They used words like choice and best option, language that suggested participation where there had been none. It was easier, I think, to believe that I had agreed somehow, that I had understood, consented, and accepted. The alternative would have required confronting a more uncomfortable truth: that a child had been carried along by adult fear and adult urgency.

I did not experience it as a choice.

I experienced it as inevitability.

From the moment the secret surfaced, the path forward narrowed with alarming speed. There were no branching possibilities, no space for questions that belonged to me. Everything moved quickly, deliberately, as if slowing down might invite doubt. Decisions were made in quieter rooms, spoken aloud only after they were already settled.

I learned then how powerless a child can be in a room full of certainty.

When I tried to imagine saying no, my thoughts stopped short. No did not exist as an option. It wasn't part of the conversation. The consequences of resistance were implied rather than stated: exposure, disruption, and collapse. I had already been taught my role: to keep things intact, to avoid making things harder, to absorb what needed absorbing.

So, I complied.

Compliance can look calm from the outside. It can resemble maturity, even strength. Inside, it felt like a disappearance. Like watching something happen to someone else while knowing that person was supposed to be me.

Afterward, adults expected closure.

They spoke as if the problem had been resolved, as if sealing one door erased everything that had led to it. Life resumed its rhythm with unsettling speed, school, routines, expectations, and the quiet insistence that we move on.

But there is no moving on from something you were never allowed to fully experience in the first place.

I was praised, subtly, for how well I handled things. For being strong. For not making a scene. For understanding what was at stake. Those words settled heavily in my chest. They confirmed what I had already begun to believe: that my worth was tied to how quietly I endured.

Strength, I learned, meant silence.

No one asked what I needed. No one asked what I was grieving. Grief would have complicated the story. It would have required acknowledgment, and acknowledgment threatened the fragile balance everyone was trying to preserve.

So, I learned to grieve alone, without language, without witnesses.

The idea that it had been my choice followed me for years. It surfaced in moments when my pain felt confusing, when my reactions seemed excessive even to me. *You agreed*, a voice would whisper. *You didn't fight.*

It took a long time to understand this truth: children are not responsible for resisting decisions they were never empowered to influence.

At the time, I believed the adults. I believed I had done the right thing. That my obedience had prevented harm. That any lingering sadness or anger was a personal failing rather than a natural response to loss.

That belief shaped me.

It taught me to accept outcomes without questioning the process. To confuse resignation with resilience. To mistake obedience for morality.

It taught me that my body, my future, and my autonomy were negotiable if the stakes felt high enough to someone else.

At that age, I only knew that something precious had been taken in the name of protection, and that I was expected to be grateful for it. One of the people meant to keep me safe did so without ever knowing the cost, and I loved him for that. With the other, protection came with conditions, quiet ones, carefully explained, and something inside me learned to close a door. What I didn't understand then was how secrecy could change a relationship even when love remained.

The decision that was never mine became a template. I carried it into other relationships, other moments where my needs conflicted with someone else's comfort. I learned to yield first. To accommodate. To tell myself that wanting more was selfish, dangerous, and disruptive.

It would take years, decades, to fully understand what I could not know then:

A decision made under pressure is not a choice. Silence is not consent. Survival is not agreement.

That decision, made without me, became the template for everything that followed. It taught me that urgency outranked consent, that adult fear carried more weight than a child's autonomy, and that silence could be framed as cooperation. Long after the moment passed, my body continued to live as if choices were provisional and safety depended on compliance. Every chapter after this one echoes that lesson.

Chapter 8 – The Fear I Learned to Carry

Fear is rarely born in a single moment.

It is passed down.

It moves quietly from one generation to the next, shaped by loss, survival, and the unspoken rules of staying intact. Long before I understood its name, fear had already begun teaching me how to live, what to avoid, what to protect, and what not to question. I learned to scan rooms before speaking, to anticipate moods, and to adjust myself before anyone asked.

At the time, it didn't feel like fear.

It felt like responsibility.

Fear lived in urgency. In conversations that ended too soon. In the tension that rose whenever uncertainty entered the room. In the way, difficult questions were met not with curiosity, but with discomfort, like doors that shouldn't be opened.

I learned early that stability was fragile. That what we had could be lost. That disruption carried consequences no one wanted to name. Safety, I was taught, was something you preserved by being careful, by not pushing, not exposing, and not rocking what already felt precarious.

Fear became the atmosphere I breathed. I didn't inherit it through words. I learned it the way children learn weather, by noticing shifts in tone, changes in posture, and the way energy tightened around certain topics. I learned what mattered by watching what was guarded. I learned what was dangerous by watching what was avoided.

And what mattered most was keeping things together.

I absorbed that lesson deeply. I learned to measure my reactions, to soften my feelings, to edit my truth before it ever reached my mouth. I learned that asking the wrong questions could cause collapse. That silence could be a form of protection. That endurance was often praised as strength.

Fear became instruction.

Don't tell.

Don't press.

Don't risk what little certainty exists.

Each rule carried the same quiet implication: If something breaks, it will be because you touched it.

That belief settled into my body. I learned to monitor not just my own emotions, but the emotional temperature around me. If the room felt tense, I shrank. If uncertainty appeared, I adapted. If fear surfaced, I complied.

I loved deeply. And love, when shaped by fear, learns how to disappear.

There were moments, brief and fleeting, when I sensed that fear was not the whole story. When I felt the urge to ask for more, to be seen, to be chosen openly. But I also sensed the cost of those questions. To challenge fear meant confronting everything it was protecting against.

So I learned not to ask.

Instead, I carried it forward.

Fear became something I managed, anticipating danger, assuming loss, and preparing for disappointment. I learned to prioritize survival over truth, harmony over honesty, continuity over care. I learned that understanding how something breaks mattered less than keeping it from breaking at all.

This inheritance shaped the way I moved through the world. It taught me to accept less than I deserved. To stay quiet when my voice mattered most. To protect others even when I was unprotected.

For a long time, I mistook fear for wisdom. I believed it was guidance, necessary, and earned. I believed this was simply how life worked, that safety required sacrifice, and that silence was the price of belonging.

It took years to understand the difference between fear and truth.

Fear explains itself well. It sounds reasonable. It speaks in warnings, probabilities, and worst-case scenarios. But fear, no matter how understandable, is not the same as reality, and passing it down does not make it safer. Fear felt permanent because it had been useful.

I do not tell this story to assign blame.
I tell it to name a pattern. Fear can be inherited. So can silence. But inheritance is not destiny.

What is passed down can also be examined. What is learned can be unlearned. And clarity begins when we recognize which burdens were never ours to carry in the first place.

Chapter 9 – Becoming Who I Needed To Survive

Survival does not leave you unchanged, and it is not a single decision. It is a series of small adaptations that slowly turn into a personality.

By the time I understood that something fundamental had changed in me, the change was already complete. I did not wake up one morning and decide to become different. I simply responded, again and again, to what was required of me until the response became who I was.

I became observant.

I learned how to read a room the moment I entered it, how to sense tension before it surfaced, how to adjust myself accordingly. I noticed tone shifts, body language, and silences that lingered too long. I learned which moods were safe and which ones required caution. This skill would later be praised as intuition, emotional intelligence, and maturity. At the time, it was armor.

I became agreeable.

I said yes quickly. I apologized often. I learned that cooperation smoothed interactions and deflected scrutiny. Disagreements felt dangerous, even when the stakes were small. It was easier to yield than to risk conflict, easier to accommodate than to assert. I mistook this for kindness. Others did too.

I became responsible beyond my years.

I took care of my sister in quiet ways, watching, listening, positioning myself between her and anything that felt uncertain. I took care of adults emotionally, anticipating needs before they were voiced. I learned to be useful, to contribute, to justify my presence by making myself indispensable.

Need, I believed, was a liability. Usefulness was safety.

I became detached from my body.

I learned how to leave it without leaving the room. How to stay present enough to function while remaining distant enough not to feel too much. My body became something I managed rather than inhabited. Sensations were monitored. Emotions were evaluated for risk before being allowed to surface.

This distance helped me survive, but it came at a cost. I stopped trusting my instincts. I second-guessed my reactions. I learned to override discomfort instead of listening to it.

I became quiet in ways that were hard to notice.

I still spoke. I still laughed. I still performed normally well enough that no one suspected the effort behind it. But I stopped volunteering information about myself. I stopped sharing feelings unless they were safe and shallow. I learned how to keep conversations focused on other people.

Silence became my most reliable tool.

At school, teachers described me as well-behaved, mature, and self-directed. Adults smiled approvingly when they talked about me. I became responsible, capable, and easy to depend on, the kind of person adults trust without asking questions. I absorbed this feedback as confirmation that I was doing something right. That whatever I had lost internally was being compensated for externally.

What I didn't realize was that I was being rewarded for my disappearance.

The version of me that emerged from this period was capable, composed, and deeply disconnected from her own needs. She did not expect protection. She did not ask for help. She believed that survival depended on vigilance and self-control.

She believed that love had to be earned.

This version of me carried me forward. She helped me succeed in visible ways. She kept me functional when dysfunction was the environment. She allowed me to pass through adolescence without drawing attention to the fractures beneath the surface.

I owe her my survival.

But I also recognize now that she was never meant to be permanent.

She was a response to danger, not a true self. She was built from necessity, not desire. And while she protected me then, she would later struggle to let go, even when the danger had passed.

At the time, I didn't know I was becoming someone out of need rather than choice. I only knew that this version of me worked. It kept me safe. It kept the peace. It kept questions away.

By the time I reached adulthood, survival no longer felt like something I was doing. It felt like who I was. It would take many years to understand that survival skills, once learned, do not automatically disappear when they are no longer required. And that unlearning them is its own kind of work. I did not yet know how much my adult life would be shaped by skills I learned as a child who was simply trying to stay safe.

Chapter 10 — Silence as a Second Skin

Silence stopped feeling like something I did. It began to feel like something I was.

Over time, it wrapped itself around me so completely that I no longer noticed its weight. It became instinctive, automatic, my first response rather than a considered choice. Words filtered themselves before I was aware of forming them. Feelings flattened before they reached my face. Questions dissolved before they reached my mouth.

Silence was efficient.

Silence kept me safe.

I learned how to carry it everywhere. At school, among friends, in rooms where laughter came easily to others, I remained careful. I listened more than I spoke. When I did speak, I chose stories that revealed nothing essential. I developed a talent for appearing open while remaining closed, present while staying protected.

People mistook this for depth.

They called me thoughtful. Private. Old soul. No one asked what it had cost.

Silence became a second skin—something I wore so long it fused with me. Like skin, it protected me from exposure. Like skin, it dulled sensation. I didn't just stop talking about what had happened; I stopped thinking about it in complete sentences. Memory learned to speak in impressions instead, tightness in my chest, nausea without cause, and a sudden urge to leave a room.

My body spoke where my voice could not.

I developed an uncanny ability to endure discomfort without reacting. Emotional pain, physical unease, relational tension, I absorbed it all quietly, convinced that this was strength. That reacting would make things worse. That naming pain would give it too much power.

Silence taught me how to minimize myself convincingly.

I stopped expecting people to notice when I was struggling. I stopped believing that help would arrive if I asked for it. Instead, I learned to anticipate needs before they became emergencies, to solve problems internally, and to handle things alone.

Alone felt safer than disappointed.

There were moments when the silence felt heavy, almost unbearable, when it pressed against me from the inside, demanding release. In those moments, I would imagine telling the truth to someone. I would rehearse it silently, carefully, testing each word for danger. But even in imagination, the outcome felt catastrophic.

I had been trained too well.

Silence had become synonymous with survival. Speaking felt like a risk. Exposure. Betrayal, not of myself, but of everyone else. The family. The story. The fragile structure was built on my compliance.

So, I stayed quiet.

What I didn't understand then was that silence doesn't remain neutral. It doesn't simply hold things in place. Over time, it begins to shape what it contains. It distorts memory. It warps identity. It teaches you that your inner world is unimportant, unreliable, or dangerous.

Silence did not remain neutral. Over time, it began to shape what it contained, distorting memory, warping identity, and teaching me to distrust my own inner world.

These questions eroded my sense of reality slowly, subtly. I learned to look outward for confirmation of truth rather than inward. I learned to trust other people's comfort over my own discomfort. I learned to value peace over honesty, stability over authenticity.

Silence was no longer something imposed on me. It was something I enforced.

This realization would come much later, when the silence finally began to crack. At the time, I only knew that keeping everything contained felt necessary, inevitable, right. Silence had become my language, my shield, my second skin.

And like any skin grown too thick, it protected me from harm, but it also kept me from feeling alive.

Chapter 11 – Trust, Intimacy, and the Echoes

Intimacy came later, but it did not arrive untouched.

By the time I was old enough to name it, intimacy already carried weight, expectation, tension, and an undercurrent of unease I could never quite explain. What others described as closeness felt to me like exposure. What they experienced as connection often felt like risk.

I didn't understand why.

On the surface, I functioned well. I could see it even then, in classrooms, in friendships, and later in relationships. I was capable, reliable, and noticeably restrained. I watched others take emotional risks I couldn't seem to reach. I wanted closeness, but I was always holding myself a step back, as if something essential might be taken if I leaned in fully.

I formed friendships. I laughed easily. I learned how to be warm without being vulnerable, attentive without being open. People felt close to me, even when I didn't feel close to them. I was skilled at creating the illusion of intimacy without ever fully entering it.

That skill had been honed early.

Trust, for me, was not a default state. It was something to be negotiated, measured, and rationed. I trusted people with fragments, never with the whole. I learned to give just enough to keep relationships intact, just enough to avoid suspicion, just enough to seem normal. Trust felt dangerous, even when it was offered gently.

The echoes showed up anyway.

They showed up in my body first, in the way I tensed without warning, in the way certain moments pulled me abruptly out of myself. They showed up in my instincts, which contradicted my logic. I could like someone deeply and still feel an urge to retreat when closeness increased. I could crave connection and feel trapped by it at the same time. I measured every interaction for risk before allowing myself to respond.

I was present, but never unguarded. I told myself I was difficult. Too sensitive.

I did not yet know that my nervous system had learned intimacy as something unsafe, something that happened without consent, something that required silence afterward. My body remembered what my mind had worked so hard to forget.

In relationships, I learned to provide comfort. I said yes when I wasn't sure. I ignored hesitation. I overrode instinct in favor of appearing agreeable, easy, and unproblematic.

This was familiar territory. I had been trained to prioritize other people's comfort long before I understood what I was giving up. My needs still felt negotiable. My boundaries still felt optional.

And when something didn't feel right, I blamed myself for the discomfort rather than the situation that caused it.

The echoes were subtle but persistent. They were there in my difficulty, asking for what I wanted. In my instinct to freeze rather than protest. In my tendency to disconnect when things became emotionally intense.

I could be present and absent at the same time; my body responded before my mind was allowed to understand. This frightened me, though I rarely admitted it, even to myself.

I wanted intimacy. I wanted closeness that felt chosen, mutual, safe. But I had no internal blueprint for what that looked like. What I had instead was a history of boundaries crossed and silence rewarded. I had learned that trust could be misplaced, that speaking up could be dangerous, that compliance could be mistaken for consent.

I remember thinking, even in moments of happiness, that I was experiencing life through glass, present, but protected. I could tell I was different, not in visible ways, but in how carefully I lived.

So, I kept mistaking endurance for connection.

The hardest part was how invisible all of this was to others. From the outside, I appeared capable, composed, and functional. Inside, I was constantly negotiating with the past, managing echoes I didn't yet know how to interpret.

I wondered why intimacy felt like work when it seemed effortless for everyone else. I wondered why closeness made me feel both wanted and erased. I wondered why my body reacted as if it were bracing for something that wasn't happening.

I didn't understand yet that trauma doesn't stay where it begins. It echoes forward, into relationships, into touch, and into trust. It speaks through the body when words were once forbidden. It reappears not as memory, but as a pattern.

At the time, I believed this was simply who I was. That difficulty with intimacy was a flaw, a limitation I needed to manage quietly. I had no language yet for the truth:

I wasn't broken. I was remembering.

And those echoes were not signs of weakness. They were signals, waiting patiently, for a moment when I would finally be safe enough to listen.

Chapter 12 – The Myth of Family Unity

Families do not survive by silence; they survive by accountability.

Family unity was the story everyone agreed to tell. It was repeated often enough that it began to sound like the truth: *We stayed together. We worked it out. We didn't let things tear us apart.* Unity was presented as evidence of success, as proof that whatever challenges we faced had been handled correctly.

No one asked what unity required. No one asked who paid for it.

From the outside, the family appeared intact. Holidays were observed. Photos were taken. Conversations followed familiar scripts. The house continued to function, and function was mistaken for health. If we showed up in the same places and played our assigned roles, the myth held.

Inside, the fractures were everywhere.

Unity depended on omission. On selective memory. On an unspoken agreement that certain truths were too dangerous to acknowledge. The price of belonging was silence, and I had already proven I was willing to pay it.

I watched how the myth operated. If tension surfaced, it was reframed as normal stress. If distance grew, it was called independence. If pain lingered, it was attributed to personality rather than circumstance.

There was always an explanation that preserved the story.

I learned that unity did not mean safety. It meant containment. It meant keeping everything that threatened the image carefully out of sight. The family stayed together not because it was healthy to do so, but because separating would have required confronting what had happened, and confrontation was the one thing the system could not survive.

Unity demanded loyalty above truth.

Loyalty required me to carry what others refused to face. Loyalty meant aligning myself with the version of events that caused the least disruption. It meant minimizing my own experience so others could remain comfortable. It meant accepting that my role in the family was not to be seen, but to stabilize.

I fulfilled that role well.

Over time, the myth became something I internalized. I began to measure my own worth by my ability to maintain peace, to smooth over conflict, to keep relationships intact even when they hurt me. I learned to equate endurance with love, proximity with belonging.

I did not yet understand that unity achieved through silence is not unity at all.

It is compliance.

Real unity allows for truth. It makes room for discomfort. It prioritizes protection over appearance. What we had instead was a fragile truce, one that required ongoing sacrifice to maintain. And the sacrifice was almost always internal, almost always mine.

As I grew older, I began to notice the cost more clearly. By then, I had built a life that looked stable from the outside: education, work, and responsibility. I did what was expected well. But stability is not the same as freedom, and I could feel the difference even if I couldn't name it yet.

The family did not feel close. It felt careful. Conversations stayed shallow. Certain topics were avoided with practiced ease. There was an unspoken understanding of what could and could not be said, and everyone adhered to it.

The myth demanded maintenance. Any threat to it, any question, any challenge, was met with defensiveness or denial. The story had to remain intact because dismantling it would have required accountability. And accountability would have required acknowledging that unity had been built on harm.

I was expected to be grateful for this unity. To see it as protection. Believing that keeping the family together had been worth the cost. For a long time, I tried to believe that too.

But myths unravel when examined closely.

I began to see that what was called unity had never included me fully—not as I truly was, not with my full history and reality acknowledged. I had been present, but not recognized. Included, but not protected. Kept, but not cared for.

The myth of family unity asked me to accept that this was enough.

It wasn't.

Understanding this did not happen all at once. It emerged slowly, through discomfort, through exhaustion, through the growing realization that preserving a system that required my silence was not an act of love, it was an act of self-erasure. I began to see that unity built on silence demands sacrifice from the most vulnerable.

The myth demanded maintenance. Conversations stayed shallow. Certain truths remained unspeakable. Unity was preserved not through care but through containment.

What we call unity was not closeness. It was compliance.

Chapter 13 – The Moment the Story Changed

For a long time, I believed change would arrive dramatically.

I imagined a single confrontation, a breaking point sharp enough to shatter the silence all at once. I imagined certainty appearing like a light switched on suddenly, undeniably, and irretrievably. That is how stories often frame transformation: one moment before, one moment after.

That is not how it happened.

The shift was subtle, but it altered how I understood myself.

It began with exhaustion.

I was tired of carrying what had never been named. Tired of managing other people's comfort. Tired of explaining my life to myself in half-truths and careful omissions. The silence that once protected me had begun to suffocate.

What changed was not the past, but my relationship to it.

I found myself questioning things I had always accepted as fact. Small questions at first barely formed: Why was this my responsibility? Who decided this was the right outcome? What would it mean if I wasn't to blame?

These questions felt dangerous. They unsettled a narrative that had held my life together for decades. But they also felt honest in a way nothing else had for a long time.

The moment the story changed was not when I told someone else.

It was when I told myself the truth. When I realized I had been living as if my voice were optional.

I began to see the patterns: how silence had been rewarded, how obedience had been framed as strength, and how fear had been passed down as wisdom. I began to recognize that what I had called resilience was often just endurance, and that endurance without choice is not a virtue.

I allowed myself, for the first time, to consider this possibility:

What if I were never responsible for protecting everyone else?

That question cracked something open.

With it came grief, real grief, uncontained and previously forbidden. Grief for the child I had been, for the choices I never had, for the protection that never came. I felt anger too, sharp and unfamiliar. Anger I had been taught to suppress, redirect, and dissolve.

I did not act on it. I simply allowed it to exist.

That allowance changed everything.

The story shifted from one of inevitability to one of context. From this is just how it was to this is what happened to me. The difference was subtle but profound. One erased agency; the other restored it.

I cannot rewrite the past, but I finally see how silence molded the person I have become. I could see how many years I had spent holding myself back, choosing safety over truth, endurance over joy. I wanted more than survival. I wanted to experience happiness without apology, freedom without fear, and a life that belonged to me fully.

I stopped asking what I should have done differently. I started asking what should have been done for me.

This reframing did not immediately make things easier. In some ways, it made them harder. The old story had been simpler. It required nothing of me except silence. The new one demanded honesty, boundaries, and the willingness to disappoint people who had benefited from my compliance.

But it also offered something I had never had before: clarity.

I could see now that the family narrative had been constructed around fear, not truth. That my silence had been necessary for its survival. That the cost of maintaining the story had been my own fragmentation.

Seeing this did not erase the past, but it changed its meaning.

I was no longer a participant in my own erasure. I was a witness.

The moment the story changed was the moment I stopped asking for permission to see my life clearly. When I accepted that understanding what happened did not require anyone else's approval.

It was quiet.

It was internal.

And it was irreversible.

Once the story changed, there was no returning to the comfort of not knowing. There was only the work of deciding what truth would cost, and whether I was finally willing to pay it.

For the first time, the cost no longer felt too high, and I began to imagine a future not organized around fear.

I am writing this now because silence has a limited lifespan. What once kept me safe eventually began to cost me more than it protected. Distance gave me clarity, and clarity brought responsibility. I finally reached a point where silence demanded more from me than the courage to speak the truth.

Chapter 14 – Naming What Was Done To Me

Speaking is not a single act. It is a practice.

Naming is not the same as remembering.

I remembered long before I named. My body remembered. My instincts remembered. My patterns remembered. What took time, what took courage, was allowing myself to use language that did not soften, excuse, or blur the truth.

For years, I relied on safer words.

Something happened.

It was complicated.

It wasn't that simple.

These phrases acted like shields. They allowed me to acknowledge pain without assigning responsibility. They kept the story abstract, distant enough that no one, including me, had to fully reckon with it.

But abstraction has a cost.

Without names, harm remains negotiable. Without names, accountability dissolves. Without names, the burden quietly shifts back onto the person who was hurt, because nothing concrete exists to challenge the silence.

I began to understand that what I had avoided naming was not the event itself, but its implications.

Naming what was done to me meant acknowledging that boundaries had been violated. That trust had been broken. That adults had failed in their most basic responsibility, to protect a child. It meant accepting that what happened was not an accident, not a misunderstanding, not an unfortunate family complication.

It meant accepting that it was abuse.

That word felt heavy when I first allowed it into my thoughts. Final. Unforgiving. It stripped away all the justifications I had been handed and all the ones I had constructed myself. It left no room for shared blame, no comfort in ambiguity.

Abuse does not require intent to harm. It does not require violence that looks dramatic from the outside. It does not disappear because it was inconvenient to acknowledge.

It exists where power is misused, and silence is enforced.

Saying this, to myself first shifted something fundamental. The confusion that had haunted me for years began to reorganize itself. The patterns made sense. The echoes had an origin. My responses were no longer evidence of personal failure; they were evidence of adaptation.

Naming what was done to me returned causality to the story. It was not that I was weak. It was that I had been harmed. It was not that I was difficult. It was that my boundaries had been erased. It was not that I struggled with trust for no reason. It was that trust that had been violated when I was too young to defend it.

This clarity was both grounding and devastating.

There was grief in it, grief for how long I had carried the wrong explanations, grief for the child who had internalized blame because no one else would hold it. There was anger, too, sharper now that it had a shape. Anger directed outward instead of inward, where it had done so much damage.

Naming also brought fear.

Fear of what this truth might demand. Fear of how it would alter relationships built on silence. Fear of what would happen if I stopped protecting the story that had protected everyone else.

But something stronger than fear had begun to grow.

Self-trust.

Each time I named what was done to me, even silently, I reclaimed a small piece of myself. I aligned my inner reality with the truth instead of bending it to fit other people's comfort. I stopped editing my experience to make it more palatable.

I did not announce this naming to the world. I did not need witnesses yet. The act itself was enough.

Because once something is named honestly, it cannot be unnamed.

The power of what happened no longer came from secrecy. It came from clarity. And clarity, I was learning, does not destroy the self.

It restores it.

Naming what was done to me did not define me by harm. It freed me from the lie that the harm was my fault. And in that freedom, something new became possible, not forgetting, not erasing, but finally standing on solid ground, with language strong enough to hold the truth.

Chapter 15 – Releasing the Responsibility I Never Owned

For years, I carried it all.

Every fear. Every tension. Every consequence I was told would fall if I did not behave perfectly, quietly, and obediently. I carried the invisible ledger of my mother's peace, my family's image, the fragile structure of a home built on compliance. I treated it as my duty, my burden, my responsibility.

It was not mine.

The realization came slowly, in fragments. I noticed it in moments of exhaustion, when my body finally protested, when my mind whispered questions that had been forbidden: *Why am I always the one who keeps the balance? Why is my pain negotiable? Why do I apologize for things that aren't my fault?*

These questions were radical. Dangerous, in their own quiet way. Because asking them meant recognizing that I had been carrying weight that belonged elsewhere. That the outcomes I had been protecting were not my responsibility to begin with.

Releasing responsibility was not simple.

I had practiced it for survival, yes, silence, obedience, adaptation, but those forms of compliance were survival, not freedom. Releasing responsibility meant dismantling the invisible contracts I had signed with my own fear and guilt. It meant refusing to be the keeper of other people's happiness at the expense of my own. It meant understanding that love, true love, does not demand sacrifice of self.

It began with small acts.

I allowed myself to notice discomfort without immediately correcting it. I allowed myself to express an opinion without self-censoring. I stopped apologizing reflexively for existing. I began to see that what I had been taught to protect—the image of a family, the comfort of adults, was not more important than my own well-being.

It was liberating and terrifying.

Liberation carried echoes of guilt because I had believed, for so long, that responsibility was proof of love. I had equated endurance with worth, silence with loyalty. Letting go of responsibility felt like a betrayal. But slowly, I began to see the truth: the real betrayal had been in accepting responsibility that never belonged to me.

Releasing it did not mean erasing what happened.

It did not mean forgetting, forgiving, or excusing. It meant relocating the weight. It meant placing it where it rightly belonged, with those who created the harm, not with the one who endured it. It meant recognizing my own life, my own body, my own voice as sovereign.

And with that recognition, I began to breathe differently.

The muscles that had tightened for decades began to loosen. My mind stopped running constant calculations of how to maintain peace. My heart allowed itself space to want. My voice discovered it could exist without immediately serving someone else.

The responsibility I had never owned was finally released.

And in letting it go, I discovered something I had almost forgotten: that survival does not require carrying the weight of others' mistakes. That endurance is not the same as obligation. That being alive does not mean being a custodian of everyone else's comfort.

For the first time in my life, I understood that I had been free all along, it was only a matter of claiming it.

Healing did not erase the past; it changed how much power it held. Some days, healing looked like rest. Other days, it looked like a refusal. The most important thing was that I was learning that healing did not require silence.

Chapter 16 – Speaking Without Permission

For most of my life, speaking felt like a risk.

Every word carried weight. Every disclosure could tip the balance. Every question, every revelation, every expression of need was measured against an invisible ledger of consequences. I had learned early that my voice belonged to someone else before it belonged to me.

Then something shifted.

It began with a quiet defiance, almost imperceptible at first. A thought that whispered: I can say this. I do not need permission. Saying it aloud felt unfamiliar, uncomfortable, but it was also electric. Dangerous in the way freedom always is.

Speaking without permission did not require shouting. It did not require confrontation. It required honesty. It required allowing my voice to exist in the world without waiting for approval. Without anticipating judgment. Without calculating safety.

At first, it felt selfish. I expected others to recoil. I expected backlash. But what I discovered instead was something I had long forgotten: my words carry weight because they are mine. Not because they preserve peace, not because they smooth tension, not because they protect anyone else.

They carry weight because they are true.

I began to experiment. Small admissions. Minor confessions. Thoughts spoken aloud in rooms where silence had long reigned. Each one was an act of reclamation. Each one chipped away at the structure of fear I had carried for so long.

It was terrifying and liberating in equal measure.

The echoes of my past, shame, obedience, and conditioned silence still lingered. They tried to make me retract, to apologize for my very presence in conversations that weren't about survival. But the more I practiced speaking without permission, the more I realized that these echoes had no authority over my present self.

I did not need their permission to exist, to speak, or to name my own truth.

Speaking without permission became a declaration:

I am here. My experience matters. My voice matters. My story matters.

It did not erase the past. It did not undo the silences, the concealments, the years of restraint. But it began to build a new foundation, one in which my words, my body, and my choices belonged to me first, not to anyone else.

For the first time, I realized that language itself could be a form of liberation. And that liberation did not ask for permission.

I am living a life no longer governed by silence. What remains matters more than what was lost. This story shaped me, but it no longer defines me. I choose differently now. I speak sooner. I leave situations that require my silence.

Epilogue – Owning My Story

It took decades to reach this point, a slow, uneven accumulation of clarity, courage, and trust in myself. The journey was not linear. It was full of backtracking, reliving, doubting, and relearning what it meant to exist in a body and mind that had once been trained to disappear.

Now, I understand that the story I carry is not defined by the harm done to me, nor by the silence I was forced to endure. It is defined by survival, resilience, and the gradual reclamation of autonomy that was always mine, even when it was denied.

I speak openly now. I set boundaries without apology. I recognize the echoes that follow me, and I meet them with awareness instead of fear. I no longer allow the past to dictate my consent, my comfort, or my voice.

The secret that once rewrote my body no longer controls it. The silence that became my second skin has been peeled back, layer by layer, replaced by language, understanding, and permission, from myself, to exist fully.

I have learned that naming is powerful, that boundaries are sacred, and that the responsibility I was taught to carry was never mine to bear. That freedom begins when you stop protecting others from the truth at the cost of your own life.

Family myths can be compelling. They can demand compliance and loyalty, but they do not define the limits of selfhood. I no longer let fear dictate what I can say, what I can claim, or how I move through the world.

I am learning, finally, that strength is not endurance alone; it is the courage to reclaim your own story, in your own voice, on your own terms.

What has changed is not just internal. I speak now without rehearsing the consequences. I set boundaries that do not require explanation. I make choices rooted in my own safety rather than someone else's comfort. Silence no longer governs my body, my relationships, or my sense of worth.

I am not healed in a way that suggests completion. I am healed in a way that suggests freedom, the freedom to feel, to name, to refuse, and to live fully present in my own life. Silence no longer controls me. And that, after everything, is the truest form of hope I know. The silence did not define me, but releasing it finally allowed me to hear myself. Silence no longer controls my life. I decide what I carry forward and what I leave behind.

Acknowledgments

In the end, silence did not win.

First, I acknowledge the child I once was, the one who survived without language, without protection, and without choice. This story is yours. Your endurance carried me here, and your truth deserved to be told with honesty and care.

To survivors everywhere: those who have spoken, those who are still silent, and those who may never tell their stories aloud, this book is written with you in mind. Your lives matter. Your pain was real. Your survival is not an accident; it is evidence of strength you should never have been forced to develop so early.

I am grateful to the therapists, clinicians, advocates, and trauma-informed professionals whose work helped me understand what happened to me when I could not yet understand it myself. Your patience, skill, and belief in truth over comfort made healing possible.

To the writers, researchers, and survivors who came before me, whose words created a path when I did not know one existed, thank you. Your courage gave me language when I had none.

To the people who listened without judgment, who did not rush me toward forgiveness, resolution, or silence, thank you for holding space instead of answers. Your presence mattered more than you know.

This book is not an indictment of healing that looks different, nor a demand for confrontation where it is not safe. It is an offering of truth, and truth takes many forms. I honor every survivor's right to choose their own timing, voice, and boundaries.

Finally, I acknowledge myself for staying, for questioning, for naming what was done, and for speaking without permission. Writing this required revisiting places I once swore I would never return to. I did it anyway. Not because it was easy, but because it was necessary.

May this book serve as both witness and reminder:

What was done to you was not your fault. Your voice is not dangerous. And telling the truth, your truth, is an act of profound courage.

Resources — Support, Therapy, and Education

Healing does not happen in isolation. It happens in connections sometimes slowly, sometimes unevenly, sometimes with help you did not know you were allowed to seek. This chapter exists to remind you that support is not a weakness, education is not an indulgence, and healing is not something you must earn.

If you are reading this after encountering your own memories, questions, or pain, pause here if you need to. Nothing in this chapter requires urgency. You are allowed to take what helps and leave what does not.

Support: You Do Not Have to Carry This Alone

Support can take many forms. It does not have to look like disclosure, confrontation, or public truth-telling. Support begins wherever safety exists.

Emotional Support

A trusted friend, partner, or family member who listens without minimizing or fixing.

Peer support groups, online or in person, where survivors share experiences without judgment.

Crisis or survivor hotlines that offer anonymity and immediate care.

Crisis and Confidential Support

RAINN (U.S.): 1-800-656-HOPE (4673) | rainn.org

National Sexual Assault Hotline (24/7, confidential)

Child Helpline International (global): childhelplineinternational.org

Women's Aid (UK): womensaid.org.uk

These services exist to support you, not to pressure you into reporting, forgiving, or explaining yourself.

Therapy: Trauma-Informed Paths to Healing

Therapy is not about "fixing" you. You were never broken. Trauma-informed therapy focuses on restoring safety, autonomy, and trust, at your pace.

Common Trauma-Informed Approaches

Trauma-Informed Talk Therapy: Centers safety, consent, and stabilization.

EMDR (Eye Movement Desensitization and Reprocessing): Helps process traumatic memories without reliving them in detail.

Somatic Therapy: Addresses how trauma lives in the body.

Cognitive Behavioral Therapy (CBT): Helps identify and reframe trauma-driven beliefs.

Group Therapy: Offers validation and shared understanding.

What You Deserve in Therapy

Choice and consent at every step

A therapist who believes you

The right to stop, pause, or change direction

Language that does not minimize or blame

If a therapist does not feel safe, you are allowed to leave. That is not failure, it is self-protection.

Education: Understanding Trauma Without Blame

Learning about trauma can be profoundly validating. Education often explains what shame tried to hide.

What Trauma Education Can Offer

Understanding why your body reacts before your mind

Language for experiences you could not previously name

Relief from self-blame

Context for coping mechanisms that once kept you alive

Recommended Reading

Judith L. Herman, Trauma and Recovery

Bessel van der Kolk, The Body Keeps the Score

Ellen Bass & Laura Davis, The Courage to Heal

Research articles on trauma-informed care and childhood sexual abuse (via PubMed or academic libraries)

Education does not require you to relive your experiences. You are allowed to learn slowly, selectively, and with care.

Legal and Advocacy Support (If and When You Choose)

You are never obligated to report abuse. Choosing not to does not invalidate your experience. If you do want information or support:

Survivor advocacy organizations can explain options without pressure. Legal advocates can help you understand your rights. Reporting is not the only path to justice; healing itself is not dependent on legal action. Your safety and autonomy come first.

Self-Support: Gentle Practices for Daily Care

Healing is not only found in therapy rooms or books. It also lives in small, daily acts of self-attunement.

Grounding and Regulation

Slow breathing

Sensory grounding (touching something cold, textured, or familiar)

Naming objects in your environment to anchor yourself in the present

Boundaries

You decide what you share and when.

You are allowed to say, "I'm not ready" or "I don't want to talk about that."

Protecting your energy is not selfish, it is necessary.

Writing and Reflection

Journaling can help process feelings privately. Writing does not have to be coherent or chronological to be healing.

A Final Word to Survivors

If you take nothing else from this chapter, take this:

What happened to you was not your fault. Your reactions make sense. Healing does not require forgiveness, disclosure, or reconciliation. You are allowed to seek help without explaining or justifying your pain.

Support exists because survival should never have been a solo task. You are not weak for needing help. You are not broken for still hurting. And you are not alone, whether you reach out today, someday, or simply begin by believing in yourself.

That, too, is a beginning.

Author's Note —

To anyone reading this who has survived abuse: your experience is real. Your feelings are valid. The pain you have carried is not a reflection of your worth.

Healing is possible, even when it feels impossible. You deserve safety, autonomy, and care. You have the right to speak your truth, set boundaries, and reclaim your body, your mind, and your life.

It is never too late to tell your story. You do not need permission to exist fully or to demand respect and compassion for yourself.

I hope this book, along with these resources, offers you a small measure of comfort, guidance, and the reminder that survival is not shameful, it is proof of your strength.

Author's Intent Note — Why This Story Is Told This Way

I chose not to include graphic detail in this book intentionally. This story is not about spectacle or exposure; it is about impact. Trauma does not live only in events; it lives in the aftermath, in the body, in relationships, and in the long-term shaping of identity. I wanted readers to understand the cost of silence without being asked to relive harm.

This book is for survivors who have carried confusion longer than memory, for those who were taught to be quiet to keep others comfortable, and for readers who want to understand how trauma shapes lives without being sensationalized. It is also for therapists, educators, and loved ones seeking language that honors truth without harm.

This book is not for those looking for graphic detail, vindication, or a single definition of healing. It does not promise closure, confrontation, or forgiveness.

It offers clarity, consent, and the possibility of reclaiming one's voice on one's own terms.

References

American Psychological Association. (2017). *Clinical practice guideline for the treatment of PTSD*. https://www.apa.org

Bass, E., & Davis, L. (2008). *The courage to heal: A guide for women survivors of child sexual abuse* (4th ed.). HarperCollins.

Child Helpline International. (n.d.). *Global child helpline services*. https://www.childhelplineinternational.org

Herman, J. L. (2015). *Trauma and recovery: The aftermath of violence—from domestic abuse to political terror* (2nd ed.). Basic Books.

National Sexual Violence Resource Center. (n.d.). *Understanding trauma*. https://www.nsvrc.org

RAINN (Rape, Abuse & Incest National Network). (n.d.). *Effects of sexual violence*. https://www.rainn.org

Van Der Kolk, B. A. (2014). *The body keeps the score: Brain, mind, and body in the healing of trauma*. Viking.

World Health Organization. (2017). *Responding to children and adolescents who have been sexually abused: WHO clinical guidelines*. https://www.who.int

About the Author

RJ Koehler is an educator, mother, and writer living in Northern Pennsylvania. Writing from lived experience, this book explores the long-term impact of silence, coercion, and conditional love within family systems—and the slow, deliberate work of reclaiming your voice, autonomy, and truth.

This is her fourth book. Her previous works—*When Love Is Not Enough, What He Didn't Break, and Life After Loss*—are all memoirs drawn from real-life experiences. Together, her writings reflect a continued commitment to honesty, clarity, and the belief that naming harm is an essential part of healing.

Her work is grounded in trauma-informed understanding and shaped by years of reflection, learning, and recovery. She believes that survivors are the experts of their own lives and that healing does not require forgiveness, confrontation, or public disclosure—only self-trust and safety.

She writes with the intention that no survivor ever feels alone in their truth again.

www.ingramcontent.com/pod-product-compliance
Lightning Source LLC
Chambersburg PA
CBHW050911160426
43194CB00011B/2369